TIME TRAVELING TO
1955

CELEBRATING A SPECIAL YEAR

TIME TRAVELING TO 1955

Author

Miles K. Davenport

Design

Gonçalo Sousa

December 2024

ISBN: 9798302725219

All Rights Reserved

© 2024 Miles K. Davenport

All the images of this book are reproduced under these permissions:

Owner's Permission

Creative Commons License

Fair Use Terms

Public Domain

All images are the property of their respective owners and are protected under international copyright laws.

Surprise!

Dear reader, thank you so much for purchasing my book!

To make this book more (much more!) affordable, the images are all black & white, but I've created a special gift for you!

You can now have access, for FREE, to the PDF version of this book with the original images!

Keep in mind that some are originally black and white, but some are colored.

Go to page 105 and follow the instructions to download it.

I hope you enjoy it!

Contents

Chapter I: News & Current Events 1955

Leading Events	9
Other Major Events	14
Political Events	19
Other Notable Events	23

Chapter II: Crime & Punishment 1955

Major Crime Events	27

Chapter III: Entertainment 1955

Silver Screen	33
Top of the Charts	45
Television	49

Chapter IV: Sports Review 1955

American Sports	59
British Sports	62
International Sports	64

Chapter V: General 1955

Pop Culture	69
Technological Advancements	73
Fashion	76

Cars	81
Popular Recreation	84

Chapter VI: Births & Deaths 1955

Births	89
Deaths	91

Chapter VII: Statistics 1955 — 93

Cost Of Things	95

Chapter VIII: Iconic Advertisements of 1955 — 97

Chapter I: News & Current Events 1955

Leading Events

Salk's Polio Vaccine Approved - April 12

> **SALK POLIO VACCINE PROVES SUCCESS; MILLIONS WILL BE IMMUNIZED SOON; CITY SCHOOLS BEGIN SHOTS APRIL 25**
>
> **TRIAL DATA GIVEN**
>
> Efficacy of 80 to 90% Shown—Salk Sees Further Advance
>
> *Abstract of report, summary of data on tests, Page 22.*
>
> By WILLIAM L. LAURENCE
> Special to The New York Times.
> ANN ARBOR, Mich., April 12—The world learned today that its hopes for finding an effective weapon against paralytic polio had been realized.

Polio vaccine announcement in The New York Times

In a momentous breakthrough, Dr. Jonas Salk unveiled a vaccine that would change the course of history. This vaccine provided a way to prevent the terrifying polio virus, which had struck fear into families worldwide. Unlike previous failed attempts, Salk's version was safe, effective, and crucially, didn't involve the risks of using a live virus. The vaccine's success was proven through the largest medical experiment ever conducted, involving over a million children. When the results were revealed, relief swept the nation. The vaccine proved highly effective, dramatically reducing polio cases and opening the door to mass immunization efforts.

The timing was bittersweet, as the announcement coincided with the anniversary of Franklin D. Roosevelt's death—himself a polio survivor. This poignant connection wasn't lost on the public, and many saw Salk's achievement as a tribute to Roosevelt's battle against the disease. Within a few years of the vaccine's introduction, polio cases in the U.S. plummeted, transforming what was once a feared epidemic into a preventable illness. The success of Salk's vaccine marked a turning point in medical history, sparking a new era of confidence in science and the potential to defeat even the most daunting diseases.

Shopkeeper thanks Salk for his discover

Warsaw Pact Signed: Eastern Bloc Alliance - May 14

In a dramatic Cold War maneuver, the Soviet Union and seven Eastern Bloc countries formed a military alliance known as the Warsaw Pact. Created as a counterbalance to NATO, this pact united the Eastern socialist republics under the leadership of the USSR, establishing a powerful bloc against

Warsaw Pact conference, May 11, 1955

perceived threats from the West. The alliance wasn't just about military unity; it signaled the deepening divide between Eastern and Western Europe, famously referred to as the Iron Curtain.

Tensions were already high with NATO's acceptance of West Germany, raising fears of renewed German militarism. The pact provided a sense of mutual defense, but also cemented the Soviet Union's dominance over its satellite states. Despite its name, "friendship" took a backseat as the Warsaw Pact later showed its teeth, most notably during the invasion of Czechoslovakia in 1968 to suppress reform movements.

While the Warsaw Pact stood as a symbol of Eastern strength, it also highlighted the era's paranoia and power struggles. As the Cold War thawed and revolutions swept through Eastern Europe, the once-formidable alliance unraveled, leaving behind a stark reminder of the era's political and military chessboard.

Disneyland Opens in California - July 17

When Walt Disney opened the gates to Disneyland, he wasn't just launching a theme park—he was crafting an entirely new experience that blended imagination and reality. Born from his vision of a place

Disneyland opens in California

where families could explore magical worlds together, Disneyland turned an Anaheim orange grove into the "Happiest Place on Earth." With attractions ranging from the futuristic Tomorrowland to the nostalgic Main Street, U.S.A., Disney's park welcomed visitors with an air of boundless wonder and adventure.

Opening day was a spectacle, broadcast nationwide on live TV and hosted by Hollywood stars like Ronald Reagan. Despite mishaps like scorching heat and drying drinking fountains, Disneyland's allure was undeniable. Walt Disney's dedication speech captured the park's spirit, inviting guests of all ages to relive cherished memories and create new ones.

Over the years, Disneyland would continue to expand, adding new lands and iconic attractions while remaining true to Walt's original dream. From its challenging beginnings to its enduring legacy, Disneyland stood as a monument to creativity, capturing hearts and imaginations with every visit.

US Begins Vietnam Conflict Involvement - November 1

US troops listen to their commander

As the Cold War tensions simmered, the U.S. officially stepped into Vietnam, sending military advisors to train South Vietnamese forces. This marked the beginning of what would become a two-decade-long American involvement. Initially, the U.S. focused on training and support, driven by fears of communism spreading through Southeast Asia. With the Domino Theory in full swing, the United States saw the conflict as a critical line of defense against communism.

This deployment set the stage for an intense escalation, eventually leading to over half a million American troops stationed in Vietnam by the late 1960s. President Eisenhower's decision was rooted in the global chess game between democracy and communism, a struggle intensified by the recent Korean War and the communist victory in China.

The war ultimately claimed over 58,000 American lives and left a deep imprint on the nation's psyche, culture, and history. Movies, books,

Helicopters land with troops and supplies

and debates about the conflict still resonate today, reflecting the complex motivations and immense consequences of America's first steps into this highly controversial war. The ripple effects of this decision continue to shape U.S. foreign policy and its understanding of military intervention.

Rosa Parks Arrest Sparks Bus Boycott - December 1

When Rosa Parks refused to give up her bus seat in Montgomery, Alabama, her quiet defiance ignited a powerful movement. Parks, a seasoned NAACP activist, had long protested racial injustices, but her arrest for disobeying segregation laws became the spark for a community-wide bus boycott. Led by emerging leaders like Martin Luther King Jr., the boycott lasted

Rosa Parks on a Montgomery bus

over a year, crippling the city's bus system and drawing national attention to the civil rights struggle.

The boycott's perseverance and unity demonstrated the strength of nonviolent resistance. As buses stood idle and city officials faced mounting pressure, the battle moved to the courts. Ultimately, the Supreme Court ruled that bus segregation was unconstitutional, marking a historic victory. Parks' act was not just a stand against a single injustice – it was a rallying cry that galvanized a movement seeking dignity and equality.

Despite losing her job and facing threats, Rosa Parks became an enduring symbol of courage. Her actions revealed the power of ordinary people to inspire extraordinary change, and her legacy as the "mother of the civil rights movement" remains firmly rooted in history.

Other Major Events

Albert Einstein Passes Away - April 18

Einstein's office, hours after his death

Albert Einstein, the iconic physicist and symbol of intellectual brilliance, passed away at age 76, leaving behind a transformative legacy in science. Known worldwide for his theory of relativity and the famous equation $E = mc^2$, Einstein redefined the way we understand the universe. Beyond physics, he was a vocal advocate for civil rights, a champion for peace, and a proponent of global unity. Throughout his life, Einstein challenged conventional thinking, resisted nationalism, and embraced creativity and human rights.

His genius spanned theoretical breakthroughs, from quantum mechanics to the bending of light by gravity, reshaping the landscape of modern physics. Despite worldwide fame and accolades, including the Nobel Prize, Einstein remained humble, famously resisting celebrity status. In his final moments, he reportedly declined surgery, stating he had "done his share" and was ready to depart gracefully. Einstein's passing marked the end of an era but solidified his enduring legacy as the archetype of the modern genius.

Einstein's casket moved to a funeral home

West Germany Joins NATO - May 6

Adenauer at NATO HQ on West Germany's accession

1955

In a pivotal moment of Cold War politics, West Germany officially joined NATO, marking a major shift in Europe's post-war landscape. This decision was not only a critical step in ending the country's occupation but also in integrating it into the Western alliance, raising the stakes in an already tense geopolitical climate. The move underscored West Germany's strategic role in countering Soviet influence, as rearmament became a key component of its integration.

In direct response, the Soviet Union swiftly established its own counter-alliance, the Warsaw Pact, cementing the division between East and West. This development transformed both the military and political dynamics of the continent, solidifying the rivalry between NATO and the Warsaw Pact for decades to come.

West Germany's entry into NATO symbolized more than just a strategic realignment; it laid the groundwork for greater European unity and set the stage for the alliance's future expansion. The redefined military landscape and the enduring rivalry defined a new chapter in the Cold War era.

James Dean Dies in Car Accident - September 30

James Dean, the young Hollywood star who embodied the spirit of rebellion, met a tragic end at just 24 in a high-speed crash while heading to a racing event. Behind the wheel of his Porsche 550 Spyder, nicknamed

James Dean's wrecked Porsche 550

"Little Bastard," Dean collided head-on with another car at a California highway intersection. The irony of his fate was not lost, as just days before, Dean had filmed a public safety message urging caution on the roads. Accompanying him was his mechanic, Rolf Wütherich, who survived with serious injuries. Dean's death was a shock that echoed through Hollywood, cementing his legacy as a cultural icon—

Dean in his Porsche before the fatal crash

forever young, defiant, and enigmatic. In the wake of his passing, stories emerged about a supposed "curse" tied to the wrecked Spyder, with tales of subsequent accidents involving parts from the car. These eerie legends only added to the mystique of Dean's short yet blazing life, immortalizing him as a symbol of restless youth and the allure of Hollywood's golden age.

First Soviet Two-Stage H-Bomb Test - November 22

In a move that intensified the Cold War's nuclear arms race, the Soviet Union successfully tested its first two-stage hydrogen bomb, codenamed RDS-37. This weapon marked a major leap in Soviet nuclear capabilities, delivering a reduced yield of 1.6 megatons during its live detonation. Unlike earlier attempts, RDS-37 utilized a two-stage radiation implosion technique, paralleling the United States' advancements but achieving it through a distinctive Soviet approach.

The test was carried out in Kazakhstan, making it the world's first air-dropped fusion bomb. Despite the lowered yield for safety, the explosion still produced a massive shock wave, leading to tragic consequences, including injuries and fatalities. This breakthrough closed the gap between the Soviet and American nuclear programs, signaling a new era in the superpower rivalry.

For the Soviet Union, this success was more than just a technical triumph; it was a significant morale boost, demonstrating that its scientists could keep pace with—and even outmaneuver—American innovations.

RDS-37 bomb loaded onto a bomber

Correct Human Chromosome Count Discovered - December 22

In a breakthrough that transformed genetics, Joe Hin Tjio, an Indonesian-born scientist, corrected a longstanding misconception about human chromosomes. While working at the University of Lund in Sweden, Tjio, alongside Professor Albert Levan, discovered that humans have 46 chromosomes, not the previously accepted count of 48. This revelation

Plate marking the discovery of human chromosomes

emerged after they improved staining techniques, allowing them to distinguish each chromosome more clearly. The discovery was pivotal for understanding genetic disorders like Down syndrome, fundamentally changing the field of cytogenetics.

Previously, Theophilus Painter had set the chromosome count at 48, a figure that remained unchallenged for over three decades. Tjio's meticulous work overturned this belief, marking a milestone in biological science. His findings, published shortly after the discovery, laid the foundation for modern genetic research. Tjio continued his career in the United States, working at the National Institutes of Health and earning recognition as a leading cytogeneticist. His discovery reshaped our understanding of human biology and remains a cornerstone in genetics today.

Joe Hin Tjio

Political Events

Churchill Resigns as Prime Minister - April 5

In a historic political moment, Winston Churchill stepped down as the United Kingdom's prime minister, ending a remarkable era of leadership. A towering figure in British history, Churchill had led the nation through the dark days of World War II and returned to power in the early 1950s. However, at nearly 80 years old and facing health issues, he finally ceded his position to his trusted ally, Anthony Eden.

Churchill's resignation marked the close of his political career, defined by his unwavering commitment to the British Empire, his oratory brilliance,

Churchill waves farewell after resigning

and his pivotal role in shaping global events. His exit symbolized the gradual passing of leadership to a new generation, while his legacy of wartime courage and tenacity remained firmly embedded in British consciousness.

Bandung Conference: Asian-African Nations Meet - April 18-24

The Bandung Conference brought together 29 Asian and African nations in a historic meeting that marked a turning point in global politics. Leaders from newly independent countries gathered to promote solidarity, economic cooperation, and a shared opposition to colonialism and neocolonialism. Key figures like Indonesia's President Sukarno and India's Prime Minister Nehru aimed to forge a united front of developing nations amidst Cold War tensions. This conference laid the groundwork for the Non-Aligned Movement, emphasizing the importance of independence from superpower influence. China's

Bandung Conference plenary session

Premier Zhou Enlai played a crucial role, presenting a moderate stance and advocating peaceful coexistence, which eased concerns among some nations. The gathering resulted in the Bandung Declaration, a ten-point manifesto promoting human rights, sovereignty, and peaceful dispute resolution. This meeting was a powerful statement by the emerging nations, signaling their intent to assert their voices on the world stage.

Geneva Summit: Cold War Diplomacy - July 18-23

The Geneva Summit marked a pivotal moment in Cold War diplomacy, bringing together the leaders of the United States, Britain, France, and the Soviet Union in a rare face-to-face meeting.

The American delegation

This gathering, the first of its kind since the end of World War II, aimed to reduce mounting international tensions and foster dialogue on critical global issues. Key topics included arms control, trade agreements, and global security.

President Eisenhower's notable "Open Skies" proposal, advocating for mutual aerial surveillance to prevent arms stockpiling, showcased a new openness. Although deep-rooted differences remained, the summit's informal setting allowed the leaders to establish direct communication, creating a foundation for future discussions. Premier Khrushchev hinted at concessions on German unification, provided it remained neutral—a proposal complicated by West Germany's recent NATO membership. While it didn't lead to groundbreaking agreements, the Geneva Summit broke the ice, marking a period of cautious optimism in East-West relations amidst Cold War rivalries.

Coup in Argentina Ousts Perón - September 16

Plaza de Mayo bombing against Perón by the Argentine Navy and Air Force

The *Revolución Libertadora* marked a dramatic turn in Argentina's history, as President Juan Perón was ousted by a military coup led by Generals Lonardi and Aramburu, alongside Admiral Isaac Rojas. After Perón's re-election and consolidation of power, tensions grew due to economic challenges, government crackdowns, and a deepening rift with the Catholic Church. The crisis peaked when anti-Peronist naval forces bombed Plaza de Mayo, resulting in over 300 civilian deaths, followed by retaliatory attacks on churches by Peronist extremists.

The final blow came on September 16, when rebel forces launched an uprising, leading Perón to resign and seek asylum in Paraguay to avoid further bloodshed. Lonardi briefly took power, promising reconciliation, but internal divisions soon led to his replacement by Aramburu, whose regime aggressively purged Peronism from public life. Perón's downfall initiated a period of intense political repression and instability, casting a long shadow over Argentina's political landscape for decades to come.

Other Notable Events

Baghdad Pact Signed: Middle East Alliances - February 24

The signing of the Baghdad Pact

The Baghdad Pact marked a significant Cold War alliance in the Middle East, involving Iran, Iraq, Pakistan, Turkey, and the United Kingdom. Aimed at containing Soviet influence, the alliance mirrored NATO in its intent but lacked a unified military command or extensive Western bases. The United States played a crucial but initially indirect role due to political challenges at home.

Tensions soon emerged when Iraq, after a 1958 coup, withdrew and forged ties with the Soviet Union, prompting the alliance to rebrand as CENTO. Although the pact focused on curbing Soviet expansion, it struggled with internal conflicts and failed to involve itself effectively in regional disputes. The collapse of Iran's monarchy in 1979 led to CENTO's dissolution, ending an alliance that faced constant geopolitical challenges and shifting loyalties in a rapidly changing Cold War landscape.

Ray Kroc Opens First McDonald's - April 15

Ray Kroc, a determined entrepreneur, opened his first McDonald's in Des Plaines, Illinois, launching a revolution in the fast-food industry. Inspired by the efficiency of the McDonald brothers' restaurant in California, Kroc partnered with them to create a franchise system that would prioritize consistency, speed, and quality. He focused on a standardized menu and an assembly-line approach, ensuring that every burger tasted the same at every location. Kroc's expansion strategy set McDonald's apart, growing it rapidly across the U.S. and later, globally. Despite tensions with the original McDonald brothers over control, Kroc eventually bought them out and turned McDonald's into a global empire. This innovative model not only reshaped fast food but also solidified Kroc's legacy as the man who made McDonald's an iconic brand synonymous with quick, consistent service.

Ray Kroc's first McDonald's in Des Plaines

Ochoa Synthesizes DNA and RNA-like Molecules – 1955 (Exact Date Unknown)

Severo Ochoa made a groundbreaking discovery in the 1950s that opened new horizons in genetics. Working with Marianne Grunberg-Manago, Ochoa identified an enzyme capable of joining nucleotides, the essential building blocks of DNA and RNA. Initially, scientists believed this enzyme-built RNA based on DNA instructions.

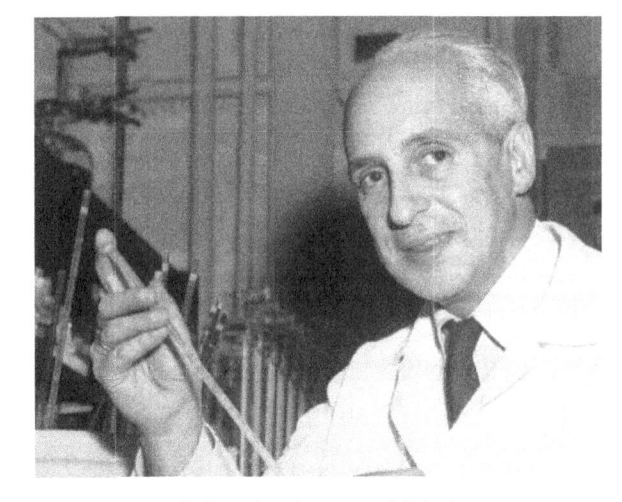

Severo Ochoa, biochemistry Nobel laureate

Although that hypothesis was later corrected, Ochoa's enzyme proved crucial in understanding the mechanisms of genetic synthesis. His work laid the foundation for future research into how genetic information is replicated and transmitted.

For these contributions, Ochoa received the Nobel Prize in Physiology or Medicine in 1959. This discovery not only revolutionized biochemistry but also expanded the scientific community's understanding of life's genetic blueprint.

First Atomic Power Sold Commercially - July 18

The First Nuclear Power Station

The first commercial sale of atomic power marked a turning point in energy history. Although the concept of harnessing nuclear energy was previously deemed improbable by pioneers like Einstein and Bohr, advancements in the early 20th century paved the way. Discoveries by scientists such as John Cockcroft and Ernest Rutherford revealed that splitting atoms could unleash tremendous energy. By the 1950s, nuclear reactors had moved beyond military applications, ushering in a new era of civilian energy.

Following President Eisenhower's "Atoms for Peace" initiative, reactor technology was declassified, sparking innovations. The United States and the Soviet Union led the race to develop nuclear power, with Britain's Calder Hall, the world's first nuclear power station specifically built for commercial electricity generation, setting the stage for widespread use. This breakthrough signaled a future where nuclear energy promised to revolutionize electricity generation, offering an alternative to fossil fuels and heralding a vision of modern progress and clean power.

European Union Adopts Flag - December 9

The European Union Flag

In a historic move, Europe embraced a symbol of unity with the adoption of a new flag. Designed by Arsène Heitz, the flag features twelve golden stars arranged in a circle on a blue background, chosen to represent unity and harmony among European nations. The Council of Europe first adopted it as a unifying emblem for the continent, with the circle symbolizing solidarity and perfection, while the number twelve stands for completeness. The stars are a nod to the ideals of aspiration and enlightenment.

This design soon transcended its original intent, becoming a symbol not only for the Council but also for the European Union. Today, the flag represents cooperation across various European organizations, embodying a shared vision of peace and togetherness, and remains a prominent emblem of European identity.

Chapter II: Crime & Punishment

Major Crimes Events

Supreme Court Decision in "Brown II" - May 31

The crowd following the Supreme Court's Decision

Following the historic ruling of "Brown v. Board of Education", the U.S. Supreme Court faced a new challenge: how to implement desegregation. This led to "Brown II", where the Court mandated that schools across the nation must integrate "with all deliberate speed." However, the vague wording left room for resistance, especially in the Southern states. Many white communities reacted defiantly, with movements like "massive resistance" organized to obstruct desegregation efforts. Despite these obstacles, "Brown II" marked a significant turning point, emphasizing the urgency of integration. The decision set the stage for federal involvement in enforcing civil rights and laid the groundwork for future legal battles that would shape the Civil Rights Movement.

Jack Greenberg, "Brown v. BOE" lawyer

By confronting entrenched segregation, "Brown II" fueled both hope for change and resistance, ultimately forcing America to reckon with its commitment to equality in public education.

Ruth Ellis Hanged: Last UK Woman Executed - July 13

Ruth Ellis, a nightclub hostess, became the last woman to be executed in the United Kingdom following the tragic murder of her lover, David Blakely. Ellis's turbulent life was marked by abusive relationships and hardships. After enduring a volatile and abusive relationship with Blakely, the situation escalated when she shot him outside a London pub on Easter Sunday. Ellis was immediately arrested and later admitted in court that she intended to kill him.

David Blakely with Ruth Ellis

Her trial was swift, with her blunt admission sealing her fate. Despite public petitions and emotional appeals, Ellis was sentenced to death and hanged at Holloway Prison. The case stirred widespread public debate and media attention, questioning the ethics of capital punishment, especially for women. Ruth Ellis's execution in July marked a turning point in British

Magdala Pub where Ellis killed Blakely

history, intensifying the conversation around the death penalty and setting the stage for its eventual abolition a decade later.

Emmett Till Murdered - August 28

Emmett Till's brutal murder shook the nation and served as a catalyst for the Civil Rights Movement. The 14-year-old Black boy from Chicago was visiting relatives in Mississippi when he reportedly whistled at a white woman, Carolyn Bryant, at a grocery store. A few days later, Bryant's husband, Roy, and his half-brother, J.W. Milam, abducted Emmett from his great-uncle's house. They tortured him, shot him, and threw his body into the Tallahatchie River, weighed down with a cotton gin fan.

Emmett Till

Emmett's disfigured body was discovered three days later, and his mother, Mamie Till-Mobley, made the bold decision to have an open-casket funeral. She wanted the world to see the cruelty her son endured. Thousands attended the funeral, and photos of Emmett's mutilated face were published in Jet magazine, spreading nationwide. Despite overwhelming evidence, an all-

The Jury for the Emmett Till trial

white jury acquitted Bryant and Milam, exposing the deep racial injustices of the time. Emmett Till's death galvanized the Civil Rights Movement, becoming a symbol of the fight against systemic racism and inspiring figures like Rosa Parks and Martin Luther King Jr. to take action.

United Airlines Flight 629 Explodes - November 1

United Airlines Flight 629 took off from Denver's Stapleton Airfield, but tragedy struck only minutes later when the aircraft exploded mid-air, scattering wreckage over the sugar beet fields of Colorado. The explosion instantly claimed the lives of all 44 passengers and crew. What initially seemed like a catastrophic accident soon turned into a criminal investigation that captivated the nation. Investigators from the FBI and Civil Aeronautics Board carefully combed through the wreckage, ultimately uncovering a jagged hole near the tail, indicating foul play.

Flight 629 wreckage examined

Suspicion soon fell on Jack Graham, a troubled man who had taken out multiple insurance policies on his mother, Daisie King, who was aboard the flight. Graham's motive emerged as financial gain, and further investigation revealed that he had hidden a dynamite bomb in his mother's suitcase. His subsequent conviction and execution in 1957 marked the case as a grim turning point in aviation security measures and FBI forensics.

The 44 victims of Flight 629 tragedy

Chapter III: Entertainment 1955

Silver Screen

Top Film of 1955: Lady and the Tramp

Lady and the Tramp

Released in 1955, "Lady and the Tramp" is a Disney animated classic that tells the love story of Lady, a refined Cocker Spaniel, and Tramp, a streetwise stray. Inspired by Ward Greene's "Happy Dan, the Cynical Dog," the film was directed by Hamilton Luske, Clyde Geronimi, and Wilfred Jackson and introduced audiences to memorable characters voiced by Peggy Lee, Barbara Luddy, and Larry Roberts. This heartwarming romance unfolds as Lady's cozy world is disrupted by Tramp, who introduces her to a life beyond her pampered existence, culminating in the iconic spaghetti scene, celebrated as a hallmark of American cinema.

"Lady and the Tramp" was groundbreaking as the first animated feature filmed in CinemaScope and Disney's first release through Buena Vista. Initially met with mixed reviews, it later gained critical acclaim, earning a place in the U.S. National Film Registry in 2023 for its cultural significance. Re-released multiple times, it achieved a lifetime gross of $187 million. The film inspired a sequel in 2001 and a live-action/CGI remake in 2019, maintaining its status as one of Disney's most cherished films. Notably, it ranks 95th on the American Film Institute's list of the "100 Greatest Love Stories," cementing its legacy as an enduring symbol of love and adventure.

Remaining Top 3

Mister Roberts

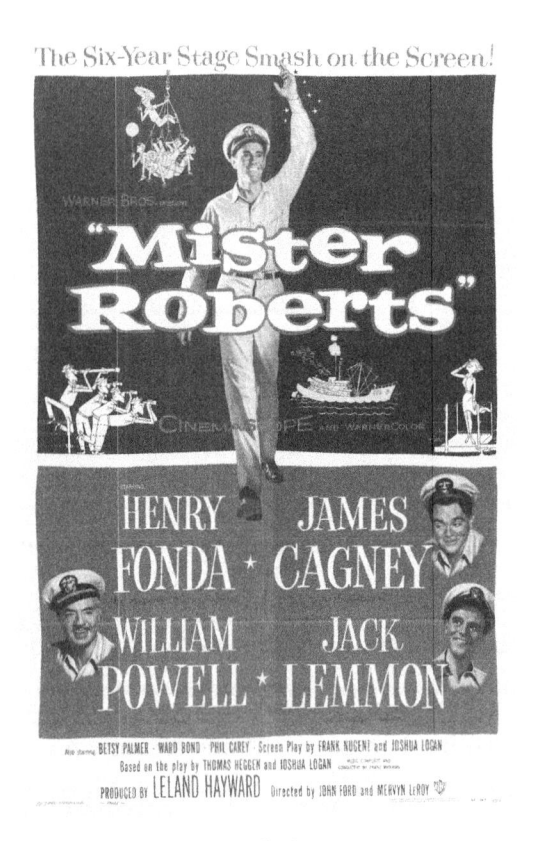

Mister Roberts

"Mister Roberts" (1955) is an American comedy-drama film that follows the life of Lieutenant Doug Roberts (Henry Fonda) aboard a Navy cargo ship in the waning days of WWII. Roberts, who longs for combat duty, must endure the harsh rule of Captain Morton (James Cagney) while maintaining crew morale. After secretly securing the crew's shore leave in exchange for submitting to the captain's authority, Roberts faces resentment from the crew until they learn the truth. Jack Lemmon's performance as Ensign Pulver earned him an Academy Award for Best Supporting Actor, marking his rise in Hollywood. Directed by John Ford and Mervyn LeRoy, the film also stars William Powell, in his final role, as Doc.

The production was challenging, with on-set conflicts between Ford and the lead actors, especially Cagney, leading to Ford's eventual replacement by LeRoy. Despite these hurdles, "Mister Roberts" was praised for its humor and depth, becoming a critical and commercial success. The film's enduring popularity inspired a sequel, "Ensign Pulver", a TV adaptation, and a 1984 live telecast. Today, "Mister Roberts" remains a classic portrayal of wartime camaraderie and the clash between duty and personal desire.

The Sea Chase

The Sea Chase

Released in 1955, "The Sea Chase" is a World War II drama featuring John Wayne as Captain Karl Ehrlich, a German freighter captain committed to evading Australian and British naval forces to return his ship to Germany. Alongside him is Lana Turner as Elsa, a spy with a complex past involving Ehrlich's friend, Commander Jeff Napier (David Farrar). As they journey across the Pacific, pursued relentlessly by Napier, tensions rise aboard, especially with the presence of the pro-Nazi officer Kirchner (Lyle Bettger), who brings discord and violence.

Directed by John Farrow, "The Sea Chase" is adapted from Andrew Geer's novel, itself inspired by the true story of the German freighter "Erlangen", which escaped from New Zealand just before the outbreak of war. Filmed in CinemaScope, the movie presents a suspenseful blend of nautical strategy, loyalty, and personal conflicts amidst wartime, capturing a tale where courage and moral choices shape the fate of the ship's crew.

Top 1955 Movies at The Domestic Box Office (thenumbers.com)

Rank	Title	Release Date	Gross
1	Lady and the Tramp	Jun 22, 1955	$66,392,893
2	Mister Roberts	Jul 30, 1955	$21,200,000
3	The Sea Chase	Jun 4, 1955	$12,000,000
4	The Tall Men	Sep 22, 1955	$12,000,000
5	Galapagos (1955)	Jan 1, 1955	$11,500,000
6	Love Is a Many-Splendored Thing	Aug 18, 1955	$10,000,000
7	To Catch a Thief	Jan 1, 1955	$8,750,000
8	Love Me or Leave Me	Jan 1, 1955	$8,000,000
9	The Trouble With Harry	Oct 3, 1955	$7,000,000
10	I'll Cry Tomorrow	Jan 1, 1955	$6,500,000

Other Film Releases

In 1955, amidst a landscape dominated by mainstream cinema, several films emerged that, despite initial underappreciation, have since achieved cult status. These six iconic movies—"The Night of the Hunter," "Diabolique," "Rebel Without a Cause," "Kiss Me Deadly," "The Big Combo," and "The Quatermass Xperiment"—have left an indelible mark on film history, capturing imaginations long after their initial releases.

Leading this collection is "The Night of the Hunter," Charles Laughton's only directorial work. Initially met with mixed reviews, the film's haunting portrayal of a sinister preacher, played chillingly by Robert Mitchum, has been re-evaluated and celebrated over time. Its expressionistic style, combined with a suspenseful narrative and eerie visuals, has solidified its place as a seminal work in American cinema, influencing directors for decades.

Henri-Georges Clouzot's "Diabolique" is another masterpiece that has garnered a dedicated following. This French psychological thriller weaves a tale of murder and betrayal in a boarding school setting, leading to a shocking and unforgettable conclusion that has inspired numerous filmmakers. Its layered plot and palpable tension continue to captivate audiences, as the film remains a benchmark in suspenseful storytelling.

"Rebel Without a Cause," directed by Nicholas Ray, introduced James

The Night of the Hunter

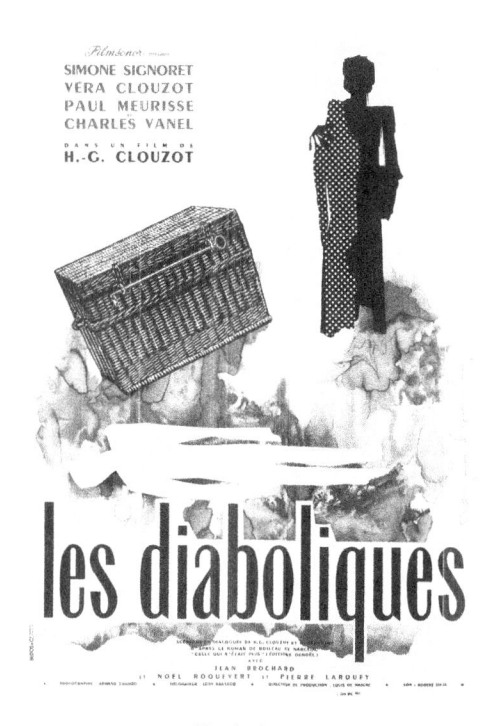

Diabolique

Dean as an enduring symbol of teenage angst and rebellion. Though it achieved commercial success upon release, the film's deeper exploration of adolescent turmoil and societal pressures has resonated with generations, particularly among young audiences seeking an authentic representation of their struggles. Dean's iconic performance elevated the film to cult status and cemented his legacy as a cultural icon.

Rebel Without a Cause

Robert Aldrich's "Kiss Me Deadly" offers a grittier, more apocalyptic take on the noir genre. With dark themes and an unconventional narrative structure, it diverged sharply from traditional crime films. Over time, its bold approach and intense storyline have been recognized as groundbreaking, ahead of its time in style and content, and it now boasts a passionate fanbase.

Joseph H. Lewis's "The Big Combo" is another noir that, although initially overshadowed by other releases, has gained admiration

Kiss Me Deadly

The Big Combo

The Quatermass Xperiment

for its striking cinematography and morally complex characters. Its bold visual style, marked by dramatic lighting and shadow, complements its tense storyline. Today, it's seen as a quintessential crime classic that helped shape the noir aesthetic.

Finally, "The Quatermass Xperiment," directed by Val Guest, introduced audiences to a thrilling blend of science fiction and horror. As one of the first films to receive an 'X' certificate in the UK, its daring content and innovative storytelling pushed genre boundaries, influencing future sci-fi horror hybrids. Its eerie premise and impactful visuals have secured its status as a cult classic. Through distinct narratives and unique stylistic choices, these films transcended their initial receptions and became cherished parts of cinematic culture, continuing to inspire filmmakers and delight audiences worldwide.

1955

The 12th Golden Globe Awards – Thursday, February 24th, 1955

🏆 Winners

Best Motion Picture – Drama:
On the Waterfront

Best Motion Picture – Comedy or Musical:
Carmen Jones

Best Performance in a Motion Picture –
Drama – Actor:
Marlon Brando (On the Waterfront)

Best Performance in a Motion Picture –
Drama - Actress:
Grace Kelly (The Country Girl)

1955

Best Performance in a Motion Picture – Comedy or Musical – Actor: James Mason (A Star Is Born)

Best Performance in a Motion Picture – Comedy or Musical – Actress: Judy Garland (A Star Is Born)

Best Supporting Performance in a Motion Picture – Drama, Comedy or Musical – Actor: Edmond O'Brien (The Barefoot Contessa)

Best Supporting Performance in a Motion Picture – Drama, Comedy or Musical – Actress: Jan Sterling (The High and the Mighty)

Best Director: Elia Kazan (On the Waterfront)

Best Screenplay: Ernest Lehman (Sabrina)

The 8th British Academy Film Awards – Thursday, March 10th, 1955

Best Film: Le Salaire de la peur

Best British Film: Hobson's Choice

Best Foreign Actor: Marlon Brando (On the Waterfront)

Best British Actor: Kenneth More (Doctor in the House)

Best British Actress: Yvonne Mitchell (The Divided Heart)

Most Promising Newcomer to Film: David Kossoff (The Young Lovers – Chance Meeting)

1955

Best British Screenplay: George Tabori and Robin Estridge (The Young Lovers – Chance Meeting)

Best Animated Film: Arie Prerie

These categories didn't exist in 1955: Best Direction, Best Supporting Actor, and Best Supporting Actress.

The 27th Academy Awards – Wednesday, March 30th, 1955 – NBC Century Theatre, New York City

♛ Winners

Best Motion Picture:
On the Waterfront

Best Director:
Elia Kazan (On the Waterfront)

1955

Best Actor in a Leading Role: Marlon Brando (On the Waterfront)

Best Actress in a Leading Role: Grace Kelly (The Country Girl)

Best Supporting Actor: Edmond O'Brien (The Barefoot Contessa)

Best Supporting Actress: Eva Marie Saint (On the Waterfront)

Best Cinematography, Black-and-White: Boris Kaufman (On the Waterfront)

Best Cinematography, Color: Milton Krasner (Three Coins in the Fountain)

Best Screenplay:
George Seaton (The Country Girl)

Top of the Charts

In 1955, the music scene marked a turning point with the burgeoning rise of rock and roll, as artists like Chuck Berry and Little Richard brought rhythm and blues into mainstream popularity. Elvis Presley's breakout success added momentum, leading teenagers to embrace this bold, rebellious genre. Meanwhile, jazz continued to evolve with Miles Davis pushing forward with cool jazz. Blues remained influential, with Muddy Waters popularizing Chicago's electrified sound. Country music also had strong appeal, thanks to stars like Hank Williams. This dynamic era saw genres beginning to intersect, laying groundwork for the evolving American musical landscape and heralding a cultural shift that would change the face of popular music.

Top Album: "In the Wee Small Hours" by Frank Sinatra

"In the Wee Small Hours," released by Frank Sinatra in 1955, is often cited as one of the earliest concept albums, exploring themes of heartbreak, solitude, and introspection. Produced

In the Wee Small Hours

by Voyle Gilmore with arrangements by Nelson Riddle, the album was a commercial success and signaled Sinatra's career resurgence. With its haunting, blue-toned cover art reflecting its introspective tone, the album became iconic, peaking at number two on the Billboard 200 and marking a pivotal moment in the popularity of the 12-inch LP. Its critical acclaim endures, ranking on Rolling Stone's "500 Greatest Albums of All Time." Sinatra's intimate and raw performances solidified his mature style, influencing countless artists and setting a new standard in vocal jazz.

Best Albums and Singles

In 1955, music blossomed across genres, from jazz to classical and the dawn of rock 'n' roll. The "Glenn Miller Story" captivated listeners with big band nostalgia, and Glenn Gould's "Goldberg Variations" set a new bar in classical interpretation. Jazz vocalist Sarah Vaughan delivered vocal mastery in her self-titled album, while Glenn Miller Plays Selections From "The Glenn Miller Story" & Other Hits continued the swing revival. Sammy Davis Jr. showcased his range in "Starring Sammy Davis, Volume I," and Frank Sinatra's "Swing Easy" brought effortless charm to popular standards.

Glenn Miller Story   Goldberg Variations

1955

Sarah Vaughan

Starring Sammy Davis, Volume I

Glenn Miller Plays Selections From 'The Glenn Miller Story' & Other Hits

Swing Easy

🎵 Top Albums 1955 (tsort.info):

1. Frank Sinatra - In the Wee Small Hours
2. Glenn Miller - Glenn Miller Story
3. Glenn Gould - Goldberg Variations
4. Sarah Vaughan - Sarah Vaughan
5. Glenn Miller - Glenn Miller Plays Selections From 'The Glenn Miller Story' & Other Hits
6. Sammy Davis Jr - Starring Sammy Davis, Volume I

7. Frank Sinatra - Swing Easy
8. Doris Day - Love Me or Leave Me
9. Jackie Gleason - Lonesome Echo
10. Crazy Otto - Crazy Otto

On the singles chart, Perez Prado's "Cherry Pink and Apple Blossom White" delivered Latin flair, while Bill Haley and His Comets' "Rock Around the Clock" ignited the rock revolution. Mitch Miller's "The Yellow Rose of Texas" charmed with Americana, and Roger Williams' "Autumn Leaves" added melodic depth to the year's hits.

Cherry Pink and Apple Blossom White

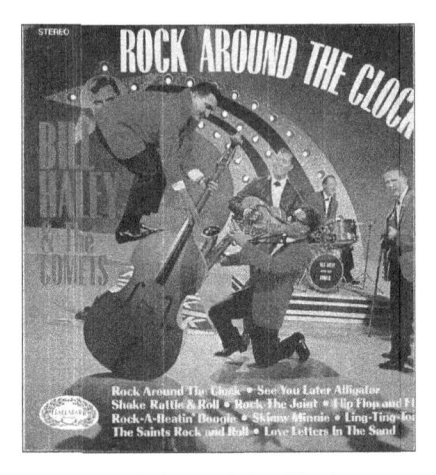

Rock Around the Clock

The Yellow Rose of Texas

Autumn Leaves

1955

🎵 **Top Singles 1955 (billboardtop100of.com):**

1. Perez Prado – Cherry Pink And Apple Blossom White
2. Bill Haley and His Comets – Rock Around The Clock
3. Mitch Miller – The Yellow Rose Of Texas
4. Roger Williams – Autumn Leaves
5. Les Baxter – Unchained Melody
6. Bill Hayes – The Ballad Of Davy Crockett
7. Four Aces – Love Is A Many Splendored Thing
8. McGuire Sisters – Sincerely
9. Pat Boone – Ain't That A Shame
10. Georgia Gibbs – Dance With Me Henry

Award Winners

Neither the Grammy Awards nor the Brit Awards existed in 1955.

Television

The Benny Hill Show

Dixon of Dock Green

1955

In 1955, television was solidifying its role as a dominant force in popular culture, both in the US and UK. In Britain, television expanded beyond BBC's grip with ITV's launch, offering viewers fresh content like "The Benny Hill Show" and "Dixon of Dock Green." Across the Atlantic, American networks were in full swing, rolling out groundbreaking series on CBS, NBC, and ABC. The year saw a significant shift, with variety shows, Westerns, family entertainment, and suspense dramas captivating audiences, reflecting TV's evolving power as a source of mass entertainment and cultural influence.

"The $64,000 Question" Airs on CBS - June 7

The $64,000 Question

When "The $64,000 Question" aired, it became an instant sensation, turning quiz shows into high-stakes primetime entertainment. Contestants faced progressively tougher questions, aiming to win the jaw-dropping $64,000 grand prize. Hosted by Hal March, the show thrived on suspense and drama, turning everyday people into national celebrities. Revlon's sponsorship proved immensely successful, boosting sales and visibility. However, the show's legacy would be tainted by later revelations of rigging, as part of the infamous 1950s quiz show scandals, which shook public trust in televised competitions.

"Gunsmoke" Premieres on CBS - September 10

When "Gunsmoke" debuted on CBS, it brought an authentic portrayal of the American frontier to television screens. This Western drama centered on the life of Marshal Matt Dillon in Dodge City, Kansas, during the rugged days of the American West. Originally a successful radio series, "Gunsmoke" transitioned seamlessly to television, where it was hailed for its gritty realism, compelling characters, and strong narrative. As one of TV's longest-running series, "Gunsmoke" not only captured the essence of the Old West but also set the standard for future television dramas.

Gunsmoke

"The Honeymooners" Debuts on CBS - October 1

When "The Honeymooners" premiered on CBS, it quickly captured audiences with its relatable humor centered around the lives of Ralph and Alice Kramden. Set in a humble Brooklyn apartment, the show offered a candid portrayal of working-class life, driven by Jackie Gleason's comedic genius and supported by the unforgettable characters Ed and Trixie Norton. Known for Ralph's explosive temper and his "Pow! Right in the kisser!" catchphrase, the sitcom struck a balance between comedy and heartfelt moments, making it one of television's most iconic series.

The Honeymooners

1955

"Alfred Hitchcock Presents" Introduced on CBS - October 2

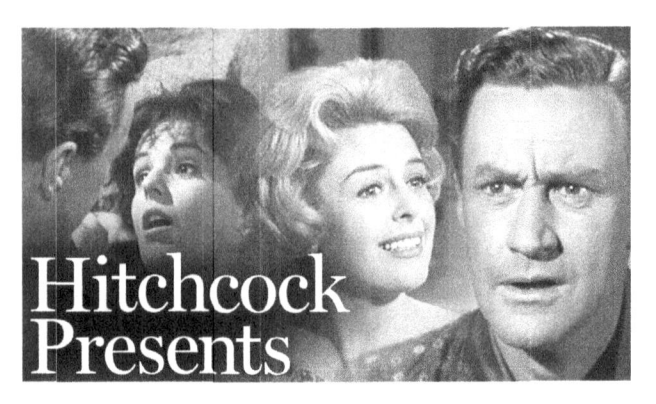

When "Alfred Hitchcock Presents" debuted, it brought an air of suspense and dark humor to television. Hosted by the iconic Alfred Hitchcock, the anthology series featured gripping thrillers, mysteries, and unexpected twists. Hitchcock's wry introductions, paired with the now-famous "Funeral March of a Marionette" theme, set the perfect tone for the eerie stories that followed. Viewers were captivated not just by the suspenseful plots but also by Hitchcock's clever asides and darkly comedic style, making the show an instant classic in the world of TV anthologies.

Alfred Hitchcock Presents

"The Mickey Mouse Club" Launches on ABC - October 3

"The Mickey Mouse Club" was a groundbreaking variety show, launching an era of family-friendly television and introducing the iconic Mouseketeers. Hosted by the amiable Jimmie Dodd and featuring a rotating cast of talented young performers, the show combined entertainment with moral lessons known as "Doddisms." Its catchy theme song and iconic mouse ears became instantly recognizable symbols. A blend of music,

The Mickey Mouse Club

dance, and animated segments starring Mickey Mouse, the show captivated young audiences and laid the foundation for Disney's future TV ventures.

"Captain Kangaroo" Premieres on CBS - October 3

"Captain Kangaroo" made its debut as a children's show with a heartwarming and whimsical approach, creating a cozy space called the "Treasure House." Hosted by Bob Keeshan as the friendly Captain, the show captured the essence of a grandparent-child relationship, using playful characters, puppet friends, and storytelling. It became an iconic program, running for nearly three decades and captivating young audiences with its mix of gentle humor, imagination, and life lessons, all centered around the Captain's warm, inviting presence.

Captain Kangaroo

📺 Television Ratings 1955 (classic-tv.com)

1954-55 Shows

Rank	Show	Estimated Audience
1.	I Love Lucy	15,135,100
2.	The Jackie Gleason Show	13,016,800
3.	Dragnet	12,924,700
4.	You Bet Your Life	12,587,000
5.	The Toast of the Town	12,157,200
6.	Disneyland	12,003,700

7.	The Jack Benny Show	11,758,100
8.	The George Gobel Show	10,806,400
9.	Ford Theatre	10,714,300
10.	December Bride	10,652,900

1955-56 Shows

Rank	Show	Estimated Audience
1.	The $64,000 Question	16,577,500
2.	I Love Lucy	16,088,900
3.	The Ed Sullivan Show	13,785,500
4.	Disneyland	13,052,600
5.	The Jack Benny Show	12,982,800
6.	December Bride	12,913,000
7.	You Bet Your Life	12,354,600
8.	Dragnet	12,215,000
9.	The Millionnaire	11,796,200
10.	I've Got a Secret	11,691,500

Award Winners In 1955

In 1955, the British Academy of Film and Television Arts (BAFTA) presented its inaugural television awards, marking the first major recognition of television excellence in the United Kingdom.

The ceremony, held at the Savoy Hotel in London, featured six categories.

The 8th British Academy Film Awards – Thursday, March 10th, 1955

🏆 Winners

Best Actor:
Paul Rogers (Requiem for a Heavyweight)

Best Actress:
Googie Withers (George and Margaret)

Best Scriptwriter: Richard Landau & Val Guest (The Quatermass Experiment)

Best Designer:
Michael Yates (For Better or Worse)

Best Personality: Sir Mortimer Wheeler
(Animal, Vegetable, Mineral?)

Best Production: Zoo Quest

In the United States, the Golden Globe Awards did not include television categories in 1955; these were introduced in 1956.

However, the Primetime Emmy Awards, established in 1949, continued to honor outstanding achievements in American television programming during 1955.

The 7th Primetime Emmy Awards - Monday, March 7th, 1955 - Moulin Rouge Nightclub, Los Angeles, California

🏆 Winners

Best Situation Comedy: Make Room for Daddy

1955

Best Dramatic Program:
The United States Steel Hour

Best Actor: Danny Thomas (Make Room for Daddy as Danny Williams)

Best Variety Series including Musical Varieties:
Disneyland

Best Actress: Loretta Young (The Loretta Young Show as herself)

Best Audience, Guest Participation, or Panel Program: This Is Your Life

57

Best Supporting Actor: Art Carney (The Jackie Gleason Show)

Best Supporting Actress: Audrey Meadows (The Jackie Gleason Show)

Best Mystery or Intrigue Series: Dragnet

Chapter IV: Sports Review 1955

American Sports

Syracuse Nationals Secure NBA Title - April 10

Team celebrates championship trophy

In a dramatic showdown, the Syracuse Nationals secured their first NBA title by defeating the Fort Wayne Pistons in a tight Game 7, winning 92-91. The game's climax saw George King make a crucial free throw and then intercept a pass from the Pistons' Andy Phillip in the final moments. The series was marked by intense competition, with each team winning their home games. Despite the Nationals' victory, suspicions lingered over possible game-fixing, particularly around pivotal plays involving turnovers that led to the final outcome, casting a shadow on this hard-fought championship.

Tony Trabert Wins Wimbledon Men's Singles - July 2

Tony Trabert showcased his dominance on the iconic grass courts of Wimbledon, capturing the Men's Singles title with a convincing victory over Denmark's Kurt Nielsen. Trabert secured the championship in straight sets, 6-3, 7-5, 6-1, cementing his place as one of the sport's greats. This win added to his remarkable season, during which he also claimed the French Open and would go on to capture the US Open later in the year. His powerful serves and all-around solid play overwhelmed Nielsen, who made history himself as the first Danish player to reach a Wimbledon final.

Tony Trabert

Nashua Triumphs Over Swaps in Historic Match Race - August 31

Nashua and Swaps on the race

In a highly anticipated rematch, Nashua secured a stunning victory over Swaps in a thrilling match race held at Washington Park Race Track. Having lost to Swaps in the Kentucky Derby earlier that year, Nashua, ridden by the legendary Eddie Arcaro, faced his rival head-on. With the nation watching, Nashua took control of the race and never looked back, winning decisively. The triumph solidified Nashua's reputation and earned him the coveted title of American Horse of the Year, while the dramatic rivalry with Swaps became a memorable chapter in horse racing history.

Brooklyn Dodgers Clinch World Series Victory - October 4

In a thrilling conclusion to the 1955 World Series, the Brooklyn Dodgers finally triumphed over their longtime rivals, the New York Yankees, securing

Brooklyn Dodgers' 1955 team photo

their first-ever championship. After years of heartbreak and near-misses, the Dodgers broke through in Game 7, thanks to a stellar shutout performance by pitcher Johnny Podres. Gil Hodges' key RBIs and a crucial double play solidified the victory, marking a historic moment for Brooklyn fans. This hard-fought win was celebrated not just as a baseball triumph, but as a symbol of hope and perseverance for the entire city of Brooklyn.

Cleveland Browns Capture NFL Championship - December 26

In a thrilling NFL Championship game at the Los Angeles Memorial Coliseum, the Cleveland Browns dominated the Los Angeles Rams to secure a 38–14 victory. Veteran quarterback Otto Graham, in his

Otto Graham's final touchdown

final game before retirement, led the Browns with two rushing touchdowns and a key 50-yard pass to Dante Lavelli. Cleveland's defense shined, intercepting Rams quarterback Norm Van Brocklin six times. With this win, the Browns captured their third NFL title of the 1950s and celebrated Graham's legendary farewell, solidifying their status as a football powerhouse of the era.

British Sports

Chelsea Clinches First League Title - April 30

Chelsea wins the 1955 championship

Chelsea clinched their first English league title 50 years after the club's founding, led by manager Ted Drake. Despite early season setbacks, including September losses and a drop to 12th place by November, a mid-season surge fueled by Roy Bentley, John McNichol, and Frank Blunstone pushed Chelsea to the top. Key victories, including a 75,000-fan spectacle against Wolves with a penalty from Peter Sillett, solidified their path. In the final game, a commanding 3-0 win over Sheffield Wednesday sealed the title before a packed Stamford Bridge.

Bentley finished as top scorer with 21 goals, and Parsons and Saunders played all 42 games, capping a season of resilience and historic triumph.

Newcastle United Wins FA Cup - May 7

Newcastle United claimed a memorable FA Cup victory at Wembley, defeating Manchester City 3-1 in front of 100,000 fans. Jackie Milburn set

Scoular lifts FA Cup for Newcastle

the tone with a record-breaking goal just 45 seconds into the game. City equalized before halftime through Bobby Johnstone, but Newcastle regained the lead with Bobby Mitchell's goal in the 52nd minute, followed by George Hannah's decisive strike seven minutes later. City's Jimmy Meadows suffered a game-ending injury early on, forcing his team to play with ten men, which left them struggling against Newcastle's determined attack. This win marked Newcastle's third FA Cup title in five years and, as of 2024, remains their last domestic trophy.

Peter Thomson Defends British Open Title - July 8

At the Old Course at St Andrews, Peter Thomson successfully defended his British Open title with a score of 281, finishing seven under par. This victory marked the second of Thomson's five Open titles and showcased his consistent excellence, pulling ahead of Scotland's John Fallon by two strokes. Thomson's steady play, particularly on the challenging "Road Hole," helped him maintain the lead against formidable competitors, including Bobby

Thomson wins second British Open

Locke and Flory Van Donck. With his win, Thomson secured a £1,000 prize, reinforcing his dominance in the sport and leaving an indelible mark on golf's oldest championship.

Stirling Moss Takes British Grand Prix - July 16

In a thrilling race at Aintree, Stirling Moss clinched his first Formula One victory, leading a dominant Mercedes 1-2-3-4 finish. Driving before an ecstatic home crowd, Moss narrowly held off his teammate, the legendary Juan Manuel Fangio. Although some speculated Fangio let Moss take the win, Fangio denied it, insisting Moss "was simply faster that day." This race marked a turning point as Mercedes claimed the podium entirely, an accomplishment not repeated until 2014. The victory strengthened Fangio's lead in the Championship, ultimately securing his third title after the Le Mans disaster led to several race cancellations.

Sir Stirling Moss

International Sports

Hungary Captures EuroBasket Championship - June 19

In a thrilling EuroBasket Championship hosted in Budapest, Hungary clinched their first-ever gold, marking a momentous achievement in their basketball history. Facing powerhouse teams, including the Soviet Union, Hungary's path to victory was a strategic masterpiece. They ended the

Soviets' three-tournament winning streak and 32-game unbeaten run, ultimately securing their place at the top. In the final standings, Hungary held strong against Czechoslovakia, who claimed silver, while the Soviet Union took bronze. With 18 nations in competition, Hungary's victory was celebrated as a historic breakthrough.

Hungary vs. USSR, Euro final, Nepstadio

Louison Bobet's Tour de France Victory - July 30

Louison Bobet cheered by his wife

At the Tour de France, Frenchman Louison Bobet accomplished a remarkable feat, winning his third consecutive title—a first in the event's history. Over 22 intense stages covering nearly 4,500 kilometers, Bobet's endurance and tactical skill shone. Though Antonin Rolland and climber Charly Gaul led in the early stages, Bobet's decisive breakaway on Mont Ventoux sealed his victory. Jean Brankart and Gaul finished in second and third, with Gaul also earning the mountains classification. Bobet's three-peat established him as a cycling icon, heralding a golden era for French cycling.

Bobet after victory

Mercedes' Commanding Formula One Season - September 11

During the 1955 Formula One season, Juan Manuel Fangio and Mercedes left an indelible mark, with Fangio winning his third World Championship.

Mercedes W196, Monaco GP, 1955

Teamed with Stirling Moss, Mercedes delivered consistent 1–2 finishes, highlighting their engineering superiority. Tragically, the season was marred by incidents like the Le Mans disaster, leading to the cancellation of several races. Fangio's victory sealed his legendary status, though it would be Mercedes' last season in Formula One until 2010. Their performance set a benchmark in motorsport excellence that resonated for decades.

Rocky Marciano Retains World Heavyweight Title - September 21

Rocky Marciano defended his World Heavyweight title in a dramatic bout against Archie Moore, marking his 49th consecutive victory and securing his place in history as the only heavyweight champion to retire undefeated. Known for his fierce resilience, Marciano was briefly floored by Moore in the second round, creating a moment of suspense for the packed crowd. Recovering with tenacity, he gradually wore down Moore over the next several rounds.

Marciano vs. Moore, Sept. 21, 1955

In the ninth, Marciano unleashed his trademark power, delivering a knockout punch that sealed the victory. The fight, postponed a day due to a hurricane threat, became an unforgettable climax to Marciano's career, ending with a record of 49-0 and 43 knockouts. His unbroken record and thrilling wins remain legendary in boxing lore, epitomizing an era of grit and power in the ring.

Chapter V: General 1955

Pop Culture

Marilyn Monroe's Iconic Scene in "The Seven Year Itch" - June 3

Marilyn Monroe's eternal moment

Marilyn Monroe's unforgettable subway grate scene in "The Seven Year Itch" became one of the 20th century's most iconic images. Directed by Billy Wilder, this romantic comedy follows Richard Sherman (Tom Ewell) as he grapples with "the seven-year itch" while his wife and son are away. When he meets his charming upstairs neighbor (Monroe), his fantasies about infidelity run wild. The playful scene with Monroe's white dress billowing in the breeze captured audiences' imaginations and cemented her as a pop culture icon.

"Rock Around the Clock" Tops Charts - July 9

"Rock Around the Clock" by Bill Haley & His Comets blazed a trail for rock and roll, making history as the first rock song to top the US and UK charts. Originally released as a

Rock Around the Clock

B-side in 1954, the song shot to fame a year later after appearing in the film *Blackboard Jungle*, quickly resonating with rebellious youth and helping launch rock music into the mainstream. This hit, which held the top chart position for eight weeks, remains an anthem of the era and an enduring symbol of rock's cultural impact.

Chuck Berry Releases "Maybellene" - July 1955

Chuck Berry's release of "Maybellene" sped through the music scene, redefining rock and roll. Inspired by the western swing song "Ida Red," Berry reimagined it as a fiery car chase and romance, thrilling audiences with its rock-driven guitar riffs and rebellious energy. With lyrics about speeding cars and love, the song resonated with teens and became a crossover hit on R&B, country, and pop charts. Recognized as the starting point of rock guitar, "Maybellene" marked Berry's explosive debut and left an indelible mark on popular music.

Maybellene

Guinness Book of World Records Published - August 27

In an innovative twist, "The Guinness Book of Records" debuted in London, capturing curious minds with world records on both human feats and natural wonders. Conceived by Sir Hugh

First "Guinness Book of Records"

Beaver and co-founded by twins Norris and Ross McWhirter, the book became an instant bestseller in the UK. By Christmas, it topped charts, and soon gained popularity worldwide. With editions now in over 100 countries, it's the go-to reference for record-breaking achievements. Today, Guinness World Records spans books, TV, and museums, with dedicated adjudicators verifying new records and securing its place as a global phenomenon.

"Rebel Without a Cause" Released - October 27

"Rebel Without a Cause," starring James Dean, Natalie Wood, and Sal Mineo, premiered as a groundbreaking exploration of teenage angst and societal pressures. Directed by Nicholas Ray, the film delved into the emotional turbulence of suburban youth, challenging traditional portrayals of rebellion. Released shortly after Dean's tragic death, his portrayal of Jim Stark gained legendary status. The film's striking use of the new CinemaScope format and its themes of generational conflict cemented its place as a cultural milestone, eventually earning a spot in the National Film Registry.

Rebel Without a Cause

RCA Buys Elvis Presley's Contract - November 20

When RCA acquired Elvis Presley's contract from Sun Records for an unprecedented $35,000, with an additional $5,000 bonus for Elvis, they secured not only his five Sun singles but also a treasure trove of unreleased tracks. At the same time, Elvis partnered with Hill and Range Publishing, establishing Elvis Presley Music, Inc., to share publishing rights on songs he recorded. This bold move by RCA marked the start of Presley's path to superstardom, as they quickly re-released his Sun singles, propelling him to greater fame.

Colonel Parker, Gladys, Elvis, and Vernon Presley, H. Coleman Tilly III, and Bob Neal at Sun

Most Popular Books from 1955 (goodreads.com)

1. Lolita - Vladimir Nabokov
2. The Return of the King (The Lord of the Rings, #3) - J.R.R. Tolkien
3. The Magician's Nephew (Chronicles of Narnia, #6) - C.S. Lewis
4. Harold and the Purple Crayon (Harold, #1) - Crockett Johnson
5. The Talented Mr. Ripley (Ripley, #1) - Patricia Highsmith
6. Surprised by Joy: The Shape of My Early Life - C.S. Lewis
7. Beezus and Ramona (Ramona, #1) - Beverly Cleary
8. Pedro Páramo - Juan Rulfo
9. The Quiet American - Graham Greene
10. Cat on a Hot Tin Roof - Tennessee Williams
11. The Chrysalids - John Wyndham
12. Gift from the Sea - Anne Morrow Lindbergh
13. A Good Man Is Hard to Find and Other Stories - Flannery O'Connor
14. The End of Eternity - Isaac Asimov

Technological Advancements

First Atomic Clock Built - 1955 (Exact Date Unknown)

Jack Parry & Louis Essen with the first Atomic Clock, 1955

The first atomic clock, a groundbreaking caesium-133 model, redefined precision timekeeping when it was created by physicists Louis Essen and Jack Parry at the UK's National Physical Laboratory. This clock used atomic vibrations to measure time with unprecedented accuracy, setting a standard that formed the foundation for International Atomic Time (TAI). With an accuracy of one second per millions of years, atomic clocks became essential in fields like GPS navigation and scientific research. By redefining the second in the International System of Units, this innovation paved the way for synchronized global timekeeping and technological advancements in various fields.

ENIAC Computer Deactivated - October 2

After nearly a decade of service, the pioneering ENIAC computer was deactivated, closing a defining chapter in computing history. Designed to calculate artillery trajectories for the U.S. Army, ENIAC's

ENIAC computer deactivated

enormous 30-ton structure housed 18,000 vacuum tubes and performed calculations thousands of times faster than previous mechanical machines. Beyond its military applications, ENIAC contributed to atomic research and inspired the evolution of programmable computers. As a forebear of modern computing, ENIAC laid the groundwork for digital innovation and revolutionized approaches to scientific and military problem-solving.

Velcro Patented by George de Mestral - 1955 (Exact Date Unknown)

Swiss engineer George de Mestral's invention of Velcro started with an observation from a hunting trip: burdock burrs clinging to his clothing and his dog's fur. Under a microscope, he discovered tiny hooks on the burrs that latched onto fabric loops, which inspired him to recreate this design. After nearly a decade of refining materials like nylon and developing a mechanized process, he perfected the hook-and-loop fastener, patenting it as Velcro. Though met with initial skepticism, Velcro's early success in aerospace changed how astronauts suited up, setting the stage for its diverse applications across industries.

George de Mestral with his Velcro

First Domestic Microwave Oven Introduced - October 25

Raytheon's Radarange technology, initially developed for military radar, led to the first domestic microwave oven—a colossal device weighing 750 pounds and priced at over $1,000. Though impractical for most households due to its size and cost, this kitchen innovation marked the dawn of a culinary revolution. Using electromagnetic waves to heat food from the inside out, it introduced unprecedented cooking speed and convenience. Eventually, the microwave's advantages won over consumers, leading to compact, affordable countertop models that reshaped kitchens worldwide in the following decades.

Radarange III debuted in 1955 and was sold in limited quantities to restaurants

First Modern Cable-Stayed Bridge Completed - 1955 (Exact Date Unknown)

Sweden's Strömsund Bridge set a new standard in engineering as the first modern cable-stayed bridge. Designed by Franz Dischinger, this bridge's innovative structure used cables anchored directly to its towers, channeling the deck's weight efficiently in a fan-like pattern. Unlike traditional suspension bridges, it minimized the need for massive anchor points, offering a sturdy yet economical solution for mid-sized spans. This achievement showcased a combination of strength and elegance that would inspire future iconic cable-stayed bridges across the globe.

Strömsund Bridge, eastern view

Hovercraft Design Patented - December 12

Christopher Cockerell and the Hovercraft

British engineer Christopher Cockerell's patent for the modern hovercraft design opened new frontiers in transportation. This invention used air pressure to lift itself, moving over water, land, and other surfaces without the need for wheels or propellers. Cockerell's innovative "momentum curtain" idea, derived from experiments with tin cans and a hairdryer, brought to life a vehicle that could traverse complex terrains with ease. Quickly adopted for military, commercial, and rescue uses, the hovercraft remains a remarkable feat of engineering, merging creativity with practicality in a true amphibious marvel.

Fashion

Fashion in 1955 was a harmonious blend of post-war elegance and emerging modernity, reflecting societal shifts and technological advancements. This year saw a preference for high-quality fabrics like wool, silk, cotton, and nylon, emphasizing both luxury and practicality.

Men's fashion in '55

Women's fashion in '55

'55 fashion store for guys

Women embraced a silhouette that highlighted femininity and grace. Christian Dior's "New Look," introduced in 1947, continued to influence fashion with its cinched waists and full skirts. Tea-length swing dresses, often adorned with petticoats for added fullness, were popular for both day and evening wear. The shirtwaist dress, featuring a button-down bodice and a flared skirt, became a wardrobe staple, offering versatility and comfort.

Tailored suits with pencil skirts and fitted jackets were favored for

Vintage '55 Dresses

Shirtwaist dress

The New Look by Christian Dior

professional settings, reflecting a growing acceptance of women in the workforce. Fabrics such as tweed and wool were commonly used, providing both style and durability. The sheath dress, or pencil dress, offered a sleek alternative, emphasizing a woman's natural curves.

Outerwear included swing coats and trench coats, often in neutral tones, providing both warmth and style. Knitwear, such as twin-set cardigan sweaters, was popular for layering, adding both comfort and elegance to everyday attire.

Men's fashion in 1955 was characterized by a return to classic tailoring and a refined silhouette. Suits featured broad shoulders, narrow waists, and tapered trousers, reflecting a masculine yet elegant aesthetic. Single-breasted jackets with notched lapels were

Swing Coat

standard, often paired with slim ties.

Casual wear included sport coats in materials like tweed and corduroy, paired with slacks or pleated trousers. Knitwear, such as V-neck sweaters and cardigans, was layered over dress shirts, offering a relaxed yet polished look. The influence of American culture introduced denim jeans as casual attire, though they were primarily associated with youth and leisure activities.

Accessories played a significant role in completing the 1955 look. Women favored gloves, hats, and pearl jewelry to complement their outfits. Small hats, such as pillbox styles, and headscarves were popular

Suits with broad shoulders typical of the '50s

'50s Knitting Knit Tweed Shawl Collar Cardigan

'50s Women's Gloves: A Symbol of Elegance and Etiquette

'50s Men's Hats Styles

choices. Footwear included kitten heels, saddle shoes, and stiletto heels, with designs that emphasized both style and comfort.

Men's accessories included fedoras, pocket squares, and cufflinks, adding a touch of sophistication to their attire. Footwear ranged from polished leather oxfords for formal occasions to loafers and brogues for casual wear. The use of color in men's fashion was generally conservative, with shades of gray, brown, and navy dominating.

The youth culture of 1955 began to challenge traditional fashion norms. The "greaser" look, popularized by figures like Marlon Brando, featured leather jackets, white T-shirts, and denim jeans, symbolizing rebellion and a break from conventional styles. For young women, poodle skirts paired with fitted blouses and cardigans became a popular trend, especially among teenagers.

In essence, 1955's fashion was a captivating fusion of classic elegance and emerging trends. The interplay of traditional tailoring, feminine silhouettes, and the beginnings of youth-driven styles made 1955 a memorable year in fashion history, leaving an indelible mark on the era's style.

James Dean: Defining '50s Fashion Elegance

Cars

In 1955, the automotive industry experienced a period of remarkable growth and innovation, reflecting the post-war economic boom and a burgeoning consumer market. This era was characterized by the introduction of iconic models, advancements in automotive design, and a surge in car ownership. Manufacturers focused on style, performance, and comfort, leading to a diverse range of vehicles that catered to various consumer preferences.

Top Selling Cars

U.S.A

1955 Chevrolet Bel Air

1955 Ford Fairlane

1955 Plymouth Plaza

In the United States, the Chevrolet Bel Air emerged as a top seller, symbolizing the era's automotive style with its distinctive design and performance. The Ford Fairlane also gained popularity, offering a blend of luxury and affordability that appealed to a broad consumer base. The Plymouth Plaza maintained strong sales, reflecting the brand's reputation for reliability and value. These models highlighted the American consumer's growing demand for stylish and dependable vehicles.

U. K.

In the United Kingdom, the Morris Minor continued its dominance, with approximately 1.3 million units produced by 1956, making it one of the best-selling British cars of the 1950s. The Austin A30/35 series also saw significant sales, offering compact and economical options for British drivers. The Ford Anglia gained popularity, known for its distinctive styling and practicality. These models underscored the British automotive industry's focus on compact, efficient vehicles suited to the country's driving conditions.

1955 Morris Minor

1955 Austin A30

1955 Austin A35

1955 Ford Anglia

Fastest Car

The 1955 Mercedes-Benz 300SL Gullwing stood out as one of the fastest and most notable cars of the year. Equipped with a 3.0-liter inline-six engine

1955 Mercedes-Benz 300SL Gullwing

producing 215 horsepower, it achieved a top speed of approximately 161 mph (259.1 km/h), setting a new standard for performance and design. Its distinctive gullwing doors and advanced engineering made it an icon of automotive excellence.

Most Expensive American Car of 1955

The 1955 Cadillac Eldorado was among the most luxurious and expensive American cars of the year. Priced at around $6,286, it featured a 270-horsepower V8 engine, advanced power accessories, and premium materials, embodying the pinnacle of American automotive luxury and craftsmanship.

1955 Cadillac Eldorado

Most Powerful Muscle Car of 1955

While the term "muscle car" became popular in the 1960s, the 1955 Chrysler C-300 is often regarded as one of the earliest examples. It was equipped with a 5.4-liter Hemi V8 engine producing 300 horsepower, making it the most powerful American production car at the time. Its performance capabilities laid the groundwork for the muscle car era that would follow.

In conclusion, 1955 was a pivotal year for the automotive industry, marked by significant advancements in design, performance, and consumer choice. The year's developments set the stage for future innovations and solidified the automobile's role as a central element of modern life.

1955 Chrysler C-300

Popular Recreation

In 1955, the optimism and economic prosperity of the post-war era fostered a vibrant landscape of recreational activities across the United States and the United Kingdom. The rise of television, the popularity of music and dance, and a resurgence in traditional pastimes reflected the cultural dynamics of the time.

Music was central to recreation. The burgeoning rock and roll scene, led by artists like Bill Haley and His Comets with hits such as "Rock Around the

Bill Haley and His Comets

Lonnie Donegan

Clock," captivated teenagers, who flocked to dance halls to try the latest moves like the Jitterbug.

Jazz and swing retained their allure, with clubs in cities like New York and London hosting legends such as Duke Ellington and Ella Fitzgerald. In the UK, skiffle music, popularized by Lonnie Donegan, inspired young people to form bands, laying groundwork for future musical movements.

Jitterbug dancing

Ella and Duke

Board games were a household staple of the era. Families gathered around classics like Monopoly and Scrabble. In the UK, Cluedo (known as Clue in the US) engaged players in solving fictional mysteries. Model building became a popular indoor hobby, with enthusiasts constructing scale replicas of airplanes, ships, and trains, reflecting a fascination with engineering. Train sets, such as those by Hornby, allowed hobbyists to create intricate layouts, combining creativity with technical skill.

Television rapidly became a cornerstone of leisure. In

Monopoly

1955 original Meccano Liverpool England Hornby Clockwork O Gauge Trains Canada

Scrabble

Cluedo

the US, families tuned in to shows like "I Love Lucy" and "The Ed Sullivan Show," which introduced audiences to a variety of entertainment. In the UK, programs such as "The Goon Show" and "Dixon of Dock Green" captivated viewers. With limited channels, television was a shared experience, often bringing families together. The medium also began to influence other leisure areas, with televised sports and events reaching wider audiences.

Sports played a significant role in popular recreation. In the US, baseball reigned supreme, with fans attending games or listening to broadcasts, cheering for teams like the New York Yankees. Bowling also gained popularity, with alleys becoming community social hubs. In the UK, football (soccer) drew large crowds, with clubs like Manchester United in the spotlight. Cricket and rugby also retained strong followings, with matches serving as major social events. The post-war period saw increased sports participation,

1955

I Love Lucy

The Goon Show

both as spectators and amateur players, reflecting a growing emphasis on physical fitness and community.

Outdoor activities flourished in this period. Fishing, hiking, and picnicking were popular pastimes for families seeking relaxation. Cycling gained traction, with children and adults enjoying neighborhood and countryside rides. In coastal areas, swimming and beach outings were favored, with seaside resorts booming. The rise of the automobile made

Boulevard Bowling Alley Union Blvd, 1955

Baltimore County picnic, Bay Shore Park, 1955

1955

The Slinky toy

Hula Kids, Los Angeles, 1955

weekend getaways more accessible, leading to an increase in camping and visits to national parks. Gardening also became widespread, with people cultivating flowers and vegetables, reflecting a connection to the land. For children, the year brought a variety of engaging toys and activities. The Slinky and Hula Hoop provided simple yet captivating entertainment. Boys often played with cap guns and cowboy outfits, inspired by Western films. Girls enjoyed dolls like Betsy Wetsy, featuring interactive elements. Board games like Candy Land were popular among younger children. In the UK, Meccano sets allowed children to build mechanical models, fostering creativity and technical skills. Outdoor games such as hopscotch and marbles were common, encouraging physical activity and social interaction.

In summary, this was a year rich in recreational activities that mirrored societal values and technological advancements. From the communal experience of television viewing to energetic dance halls and tranquil outdoor hobbies, leisure pursuits provided a sense of normalcy and joy in a rapidly changing world.

Chapter VI: Births & Deaths 1955

Births (onthisday.com)

January 6 – Rowan Atkinson: English Actor and Comedian

January 9 – J.K. Simmons: American Actor

January 17 – Steve Earle: American Musician

January 18 – Kevin Costner: American Actor and Director

January 19 – Simon Rattle: English Conductor

January 26 – Eddie Van Halen: Dutch-American Guitarist

January 28 – Nicolas Sarkozy: French Politician

February 19 – Jeff Daniels: American Actor and Musician

February 21 – Kelsey Grammer: American Actor

February 24 – Steve Jobs: American Entrepreneur

March 15 – Dee Snider: American Musician

March 19 – Bruce Willis: American Actor

1955

March 27 – Mariano Rajoy: Spanish Politician

March 28 – Reba McEntire: American Singer and Actress

May 2 – Donatella Versace: Italian Fashion Designer

May 6 – Tom Bergeron: American TV Host

May 17 – Bill Paxton: American Actor and Filmmaker

May 18 – Chow Yun-fat: Hong Kong Actor

May 20 – Zbigniew Preisner: Polish Composer

June 2 – Dana Carvey: American Comedian

June 8 – Tim Berners-Lee: English Computer Scientist

June 8 – Griffin Dunne: American Actor and Director

June 16 – Laurie Metcalf: American Actress

June 21 – Michel Platini: French Footballer

June 23 – Glenn Danzig: American Musician

June 26 – Mick Jones: British Musician

July 9 – Lindsey Graham: American Politician

July 19 – Dalton McGuinty: Canadian Politician

August 4 – Billy Bob Thornton: American Actor

August 22 – Chiranjeevi: Indian Actor and Politician

September 7 – Mira Furlan: Croatian Actress

September 25 – Karl-Heinz Rummenigge: German Footballer

October 28 – Bill Gates: American Entrepreneur

November 5 – Kris Jenner: American Media Personality

November 27 – Bill Nye: American Science Educator and TV Host

November 30 – Billy Idol: English Musician

Deaths (onthisday.com)

January 2nd – José Antonio Remón Cantera: Panamanian President

January 21st – Archie Hahn: American Olympic Sprinter

January 24th – Ira Hayes: American Marine and Iwo Jima Flag Raiser

February 20th – Oswald Avery: American Medical Researcher

February 23rd – Paul Claudel: French Poet and Diplomat

February 27th – Trixie Friganza: American Actress

1955

March 9th – Matthew Henson: American Explorer

March 11th – Alexander Fleming: Scottish Bacteriologist

March 12th – Charlie Parker: American Jazz Saxophonist

March 19th – Mihály Károlyi: Hungarian Politician

April 18th – Albert Einstein: German-born Physicist

May 4th – George Enescu: Romanian Composer

July 13th – Ruth Ellis: British Convicted Murderer

August 2nd – Wallace Stevens: American Poet

August 5th – Carmen Miranda: Brazilian Singer and Actress

August 12th – Thomas Mann: German Novelist

August 28th – Emmett Till: African American Murder Victim

September 30th – James Dean: American Actor

October 25th – Sadako Sasaki: Japanese Atomic Bomb Victim

November 4th – Cy Young: American Baseball Pitcher

November 5th – Maurice Utrillo: French Painter

November 14th – Robert E. Sherwood: American Playwright

Chapter VII: Statistics 1955

GDP

- U.S. GDP 1955 – $414.8 billion (multpl.com)
- U.S. GDP 2023 – $27.36 trillion (worldbank.org)
- U.K. GDP 1955 – $52.92 billion (worldbank.org)
- U.K. GDP 2023 – $3.34 trillion (worldbank.org)

Inflation

- U.S. Inflation 1955 – 0.4% (worldbank.org)
- U.S. Inflation 2023 – 4.1% (worldbank.org)
- U.K. Inflation 1955 – 3.5% (statbureau.org)
- U.K. Inflation 2023 – 6.8% (worldbank.org)

Population

- U.S. Population 1955 – 165.9 million (populationpyramid.net)
- U.S. Population 2023 – 334.9 million (worldbank.org)
- U.K. Population 1955 – 51.2 million (populationpyramid.net)
- U.K. Population 2023 – 68.35 million (worldbank.org)

Life Expectancy at Birth

- U.S. Life Expectancy at Birth 1955 – 69.6 years (worldbank.org)
- U.S. Life Expectancy at Birth 2022 – 77.0 years (worldbank.org)
- U.K. Life Expectancy at Birth 1955 – 69.9 years (macrotrends.net)
- U.K. Life Expectancy at Birth 2022 – 82.0 years (worldbank.org)

Annual Working Hours Per Worker

- U.S. Annual Working Hours Per Worker 1955 – 1,978 hours (ourworldindata.org)

- ★ U.S. Annual Working Hours Per Worker 2017 – 1,557 hours (ourworldindata.org)
- ★ U.K. Annual Working Hours Per Worker 1955 – 2,200 hours (ourworldindata.org)
- ★ U.K. Annual Working Hours Per Worker 2017 – 1,670 hours (ourworldindata.org)

Unemployment Rate

- ★ U.S. Unemployment Rate 1955 – 4.4% (countryeconomy.com)
- ★ U.S. Unemployment Rate 2023 – 3.6% (worldbank.org)
- ★ U.K. Unemployment Rate 1955 – 1.1% (jstor.org)
- ★ U.K. Unemployment Rate 2023 – 4.0% (ons.gov.uk)

Tax Revenue (% of GDP)

- ★ U.S. Tax Revenue (% of GDP) 1955 – 17.2% (taxpolicycenter.org)
- ★ U.S. Tax Revenue (% of GDP) 2022 – 12.2% (worldbank.org)
- ★ U.K. Tax Revenue (% of GDP) 1955 – 44.2% (ceicdata.com)
- ★ U.K. Tax Revenue (% of GDP) 2022 – 27.3% (worldbank.org)

Prison Population

- ★ U.S. Prison Population 1955 – 185,783 inmates (bjs.gov)
- ★ U.S. Prison Population 2021 – 1,230,100 inmates (bjs.ojp.gov)
- ★ U.K. Prison Population 1955 – 20,528 inmates (prisonreformtrust.org.uk)
- ★ U.K. Prison Population 2023 – 97,700 inmates (parliament.uk)

Average Cost of a New House

- ★ U.S. Average Cost of a New House 1955 – $11,742 (retrowow.co.uk)
- ★ U.S. Average Cost of a New House 2023 – $495,100 (dqydj.com)
- ★ U.K. Average Cost of a New House 1955 – £1,937 (retrowow.co.uk)
- ★ U.K. Average Cost of a New House 2023 – £290,000 (ons.gov.uk)

Average Income per Year

- U.S. Average Income per Year 1955 – $2,950 (census.gov)
- U.S. Average Income per Year 2023 – $106,400 (multpl.com)
- U.K. Average Income per Year 1955 – £462.80 annually (retrowow.co.uk)
- U.K. Average Income per Year 2023 – £34,963 (statista.com)

U.S. Cost of Living

The $100 from 1955 has grown to about $1,177.85 today, up $1,077.85 over 69 years due to an average yearly inflation of 3.64%, resulting in a 1,077.85% total price hike (in2013dollars.com).

U.K. Cost of Living

Today's £3,288.02 mirrors the purchasing power of £100 in 1955, showing a £3,188.02 hike over 69 years. The pound's yearly inflation rate averaged 5.19% during this period, leading to a 3,188.02% total price rise (in2013dollars.com).

Cost Of Things

United States

- Men's coat: $44.85 - $85.00 (mclib.info)
- Men's shirts: $2.99 - $3.95 (mclib.info)
- Women's dresses, "suit style": $14.98 (mclib.info)
- Women's coats, mink trimmed wool: $79.00 - $139.00 (mclib.info)
- Boy's dungarees: $1.00/pair (mclib.info)
- Fresh eggs (1 dozen): $0.61 (stacker.com)
- Apples, Winesap (2 lbs): $0.27 (mclib.info)
- Butter, Swift's Brookfield (1 lb): $0.63 (mclib.info)

1955

- White bread (1 pound): $0.18 (stacker.com)
- Coffee, Eight O'Clock (1 lb bag): $0.95 (mclib.info)
- Sliced bacon (1 pound): $0.66 (stacker.com)
- Chicken, frying (1 lb): $0.45 (mclib.info)
- Potatoes, New Crop Florida (3 lbs): $0.20 (mclib.info)
- Peanut butter, Beech Nut (11 oz jar): $0.39 (mclib.info)
- Jelly (32 oz jar): $0.45 (mclib.info)
- Fresh delivered milk (1/2 gallon): $0.46 (stacker.com)

United Kingdom (retrowow.co.uk)

- Gallon of petrol: 4s 6½d
- Pint of beer (bottled): 1s 11d
- 20 cigarettes: 3s 7d
- Loaf of bread (white, unwrapped): 7½d
- Pint of milk: 7d
- Eggs (1 dozen): 4s 7d
- Cheddar cheese (1 lb): 2s 6d
- Butter (½ lb): 1s 11d
- Eating apples (1 lb): 1s 1d
- Potatoes (1 lb): 3d
- Onions (1 lb): 5½d
- Oranges (1 lb): 11d
- Penguin chocolate bar: 3½d
- Bush TV53 14" television: 65 guineas
- Ferranti M55 radio: 13½ guineas
- Qualcast Panther push lawn mower: £7 7s 5d

Chapter VIII: Iconic Advertisements of 1955

IBM: Electronic Calculator

Quaker Oats

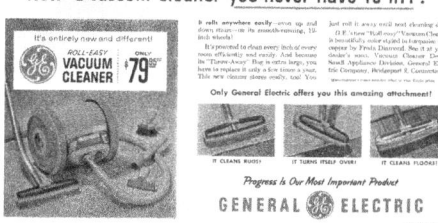

General Electric: Roll-Easy Vacuum Cleaner

Heinz: 12 Minute Meals

Kodak: Brownie Movie Camera

Campbell's Tomato Soup

'55 Ford

Chesterfield

1955

Schlitz

RCA Victor TV: 21-inch Color TV

Nescafé: Instant Coffee

'55 Plymouth

1955

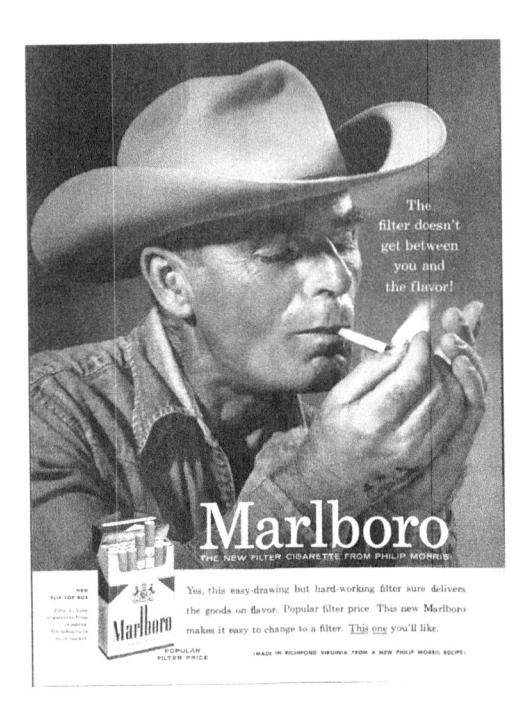

Marlboro

Budweiser

Tide

Pepsi-Cola

1955

IBM: Electric Typewriters

Cracker Jack

General Motors: 1955 Chevrolet Bel Air
& 1955 Pontiac Catalina

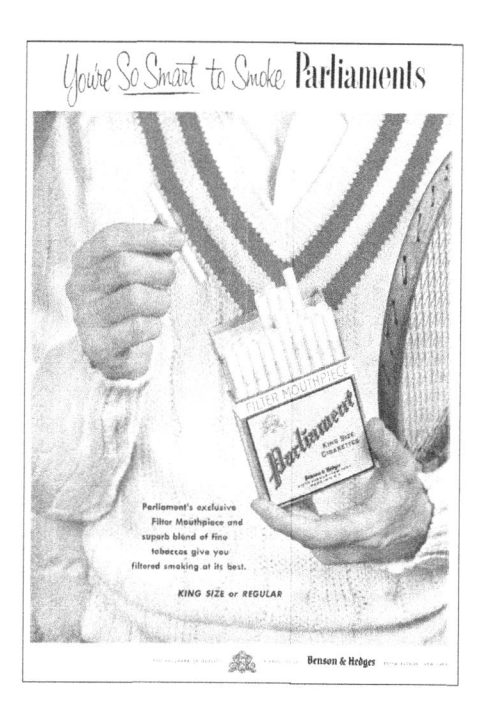

Parliament

1955

Smirnoff Vodka

Dickies

Coca-Cola

Philips: Radio

1955

Kellogg's: Corn Flakes

Chrysler: 1955 Imperial

Lucky Strike

Miller: High Life

103

United Air Lines

7-Up

I have a gift for you!

Dear reader, thank you so much for reading my book!

To make this book more (much more!) affordable, all images are in black and white, but I've created a special gift for you!

You can now have access, for FREE, to the PDF version of this book with the original images!

Keep in mind that some are originally black and white, but some are colored.

I hope you enjoy it!

Download it here:

bit.ly/4ggDD48

Or Scan this QR Code:

I have a favor to ask you!

I deeply hope you've enjoyed reading this book and felt transported right into 1955!

I loved researching it, organizing it, and writing it, knowing that it would make your day a little brighter.

If you've enjoyed it too, I would be extremely grateful if you took just a few minutes to leave a positive customer review and share it with your friends.

As an unknown author, that makes all the difference and gives me the extra energy I need to keep researching, writing, and bringing joy to all my readers. Thank you!

Best regards,
Miles K. Davenport

Please leave a positive book review here:

https://amzn.to/3CZ2Jpy

Or Scan this QR Code:

Discover Other Books in this Collection!

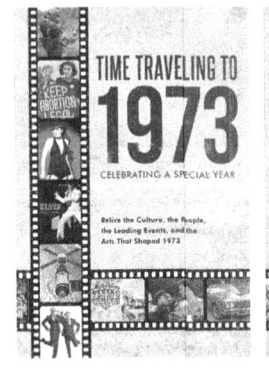